LOVE, SUNRISE,
and Elevated Apes

NINA LEEN

all photographs by the author

W · W · NORTON & COMPANY · INC · NEW YORK

Also by Nina Leen
Women, Heroes, and a Frog

FIRST EDITION

ISBN 0 393 08694 1 (Cloth Edition)
ISBN 0 393 08699 2 (Paper Edition)

Pictures previously taken for *Life* Magazine reprinted here with the permission of Time, Inc.

Layout by the Author

PRINTED IN THE UNITED STATES OF AMERICA

1 2 3 4 5 6 7 8 9 0

If there were dreams to sell
What would you buy?
Thomas Lovell Beddoes
(1803–1849)

Man alone suffers so excruciatingly in the world
that he was compelled to invent laughter.

Friedrich Wilhelm Nietzsche (1844–1900)

The capacity for laughter has never been granted to man before the fortieth day from his birth, and then it is looked upon as a miracle of precocity.

Pliny the Elder (A.D. 23–79)

I am a great friend to public amusements,
for they keep people from vice.

Samuel Johnson (1709–1784)

I've taken my fun where I've found it.

Rudyard Kipling (1865–1936)

One of the merriest things in all the world is a cat's kitten.

Irish proverb

A tiger has a natural right to eat a man; but
if he may eat one man he may eat another
so that a tiger has a right of property in all
man, as potential tiger-meat.

Thomas Henry Huxley (1825–1895)

A hen is only an egg's way of making another egg.
Samuel Butler (1835–1902)

Oscar Wilde claimed that he once saw
in a French journal, under a drawing
of a bonnet, the words: "With this
style the mouth is worn slightly open."
Oscar Wilde (1856–1900)

A fashionable woman
is always in love
with herself.
François de la Rochefoucauld
(1613–1680)

I tell you that there are terrible temptations which it
requires strength, strength and courage, to yield to.

Oscar Wilde (1856–1900)

If this is coffee, please bring me some tea;
but if this is tea, please bring me some coffee.

Abraham Lincoln (1809–1865)

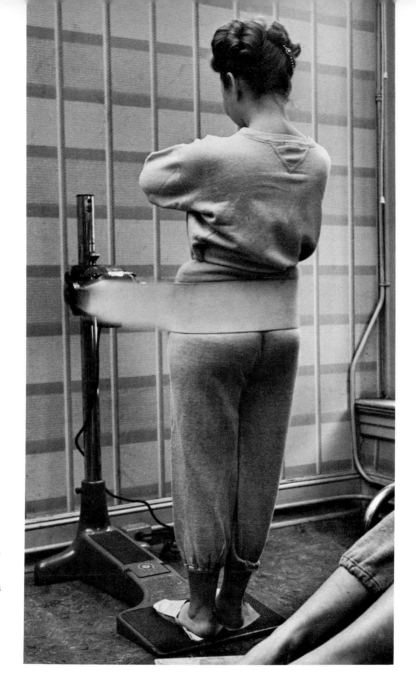

No one is free who is
a slave to the body.
Seneca
(4 B.C.?–A.D. 65)

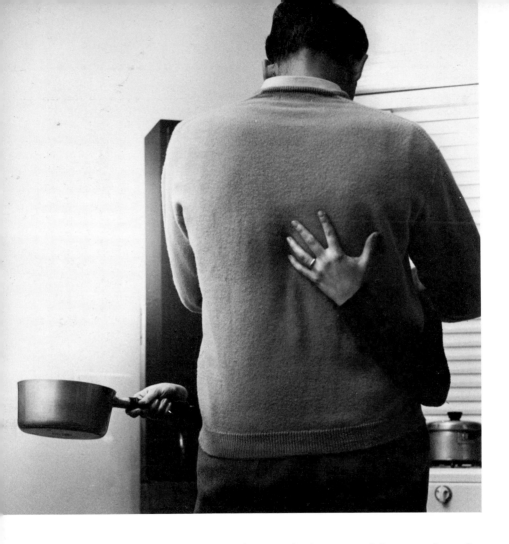

A man is in general better pleased
when he has a good dinner upon his table,
than when his wife talks Greek.

Samuel Johnson (1709–1784)

The discovery of a new dish does more for human happiness
than the discovery of a new star.

Anthelme Brillat-Savarin (1755–1826)

My murderers shall come to grief,
Along with all who relish beef;
When I'm a man and you're a cow,
I'll eat you as you eat me now.

Unknown

We are so curiously made that one atom put in the wrong place in our original structure will often make us unhappy for life.

William Godwin (1756–1836)

Moments big as years.
John Keats
(1795–1821)

The anatomical juxtaposition of two orbicularis
oris muscles in a state of contraction.

Dr. Henry Gibbons (1808–1848)
(definition of a kiss)

I wish he would
explain his explanation.
George Gordon, Lord Byron
(1788–1824)

Now I know what love is.

Vergil

(70–19 B.C.)

Complaint is the largest tribute
heaven receives, and the sincerest
part of our devotion.

Jonathan Swift (1667–1745)

God created Adam master and lord of
living creatures, but Eve spoiled all.
Martin Luther (1483–1546)

Women are not altogether in the wrong
when they refuse the rules of life
prescribed to the World,
for men only have established them
and without their consent.

Michel Eyquem de Montaigne
(1533–1592)

I earnestly ask my sisters to keep clear of the jargon about the rights of women which urges women to do all that men do . . . merely because men do it, and without regard to whether this is the best that women can do.

Florence Nightingale (1820–1910)

Are dogs divided into hes and shes,
or do they both share equally
in hunting and in keeping watch
and in the other duties of dogs?

Plato (427?–347 B.C.)

Women are never stronger than when they arm
themselves with their weaknesses.

Madame du Deffand (1697–1780)

Let's go hand in hand, not one before another.
William Shakespeare (1546–1616)

There are a few things that never go out of style,
and a feminine woman is one of them.

Jobyna Ralston

A woman never forgets her sex.
She would rather talk with a man
than an angel, any day.

Oliver Wendell Holmes
(1841–1935)

When you educate a man you educate an individual, when you educate a woman you educate a whole family.

Charles McIver
(1860–1906)

Ask'd her to acquit me of rudeness if I drew off her glove . . . I told her 'twas great odds between handling a dead goat and a living lady.

Samuel Sewall (1652–1730)

A woman . . . always feels herself complimented by love, though it may be from a man incapable of winning her heart, or perhaps even her esteem.

Abel Stevens (1815–1897)

The eyes have one language everywhere.
George Herbert (1593–1633)

There is only one thing for a man to do who
is married to a woman who enjoys spending money,
and that is to enjoy earning it.

Edgar Watson Howe (1853–1937)

People have declaimed against luxury for 2,000 years . . .
and people have always delighted in it.

Voltaire (1694–1778)

To meet, to know, to love—and then to part,
Is the sad tale of many a human heart.

Samuel Taylor Coleridge
(1772–1834)

Let us embrace and from this moment vow an eternal misery together.

Thomas Otway (1652–1685)

Experience shows that a very populous city
can seldom, if ever, be properly governed.

Aristotle (384–322 B.C.)

It is true, I never assisted the sun materially in his rising;
but, doubt not, it was of the last importance only to be
present at it.

Henry David Thoreau (1817–1862)

Who wishes to give himself
an abundance of trouble,
let him equip these two things:
a ship and a woman.

Plautus
(254?–184 B.C.)

Home, in one form or another,
is the great object of life.

Josiah Gilbert Holland
(1819–1881)

Summer is icumen in,
Lhude sing cuccu!
Groweth sed, and bloweth med,
And springth the wude nu—
Sing cuccu!

Oldest recorded English folk song,
ca. 1200

All cannot live on the plaza, but everyone
may enjoy the sun.

Italian proverb

Were I to choose a religion,
I would probably become a
worshipper of the sun.

Napoleon I
(1769–1821)

What dreadful hot weather we have!
It keeps me in a continual
state of inelegance.

Jane Austen (1775–1817)

I never expected to see
the day when the girls
would get sunburned in
the places they do now.
Will Rogers
(1879–1935)

No civilized person ever goes to bed the same
day he gets up.

Richard Harding Davis
(1864–1916)

Nobody of any real culture ever talks nowadays
about the beauty of the sunset. Sunsets are
quite old-fashioned.

Oscar Wilde (1856–1900)

The optimist proclaims that we live in the best of all possible worlds; and the pessimist fears this is true.

James Branch Cabell (1879–1958)

But suppose, as some folks say,
the sky should fall?

Terence
(185–159 B.C.)

The most civilized people are as near to barbarism
as the most polished steel is to rust. Nations, like
metals, have only superficial brilliancy.

Antoine de Rivarol (1753–1801)

We are mad, not only individually, but nationally. We check manslaughter and isolated murders; but what of war and the much vaunted crime of slaughtering whole peoples?

Seneca (4 B.C.?–A.D. 65)

He snatched the thunderbolt from heaven,
then the sceptre from tyrants.

Anne Robert Jacques Turgot
(1727–1781)
(inscription for the Houdon bust
of Franklin, 1778)

Notwithstanding my experiments
with electricity, the thunderbolt
continues to fall under our noses
and as for the tyrant,
there are a million of us still
engaged at snatching away his sceptre.
Benjamin Franklin (commenting
on Turgot's inscription)

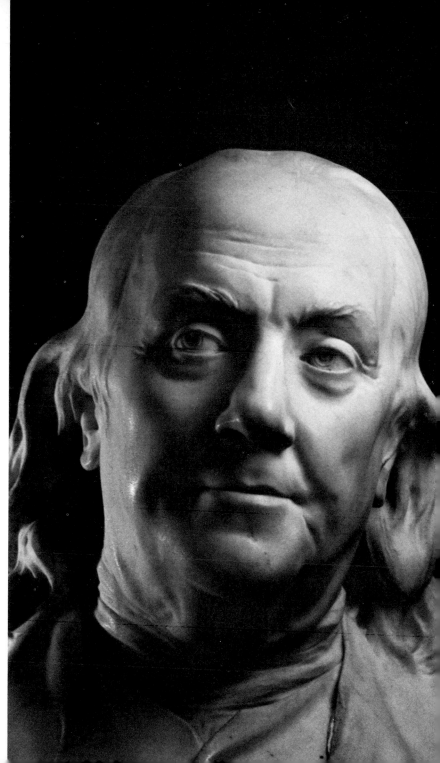

Poverty is very good in poems but very bad in the house;
very good in maxims and sermons but very bad in practical life.
Henry Ward Beecher (1813–1887)

Dogs do not dislike poor families.
Chinese proverb

Histories are more full of examples of the fidelity of dogs than of friends.

Alexander Pope (1688–1744)

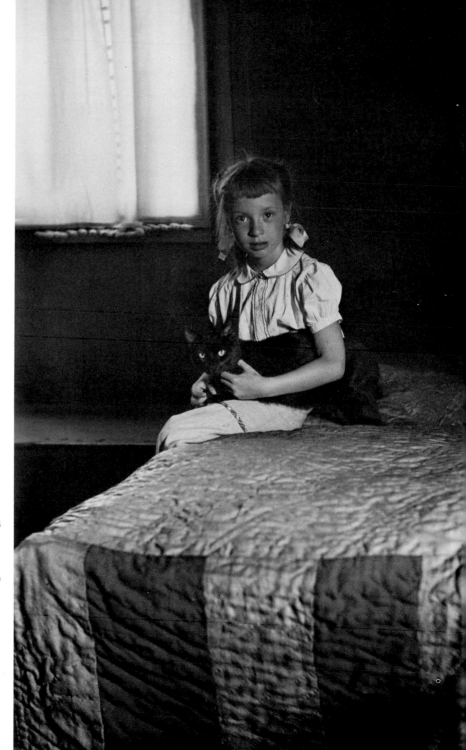

Animals are such agreeable friends
they ask no questions,
they pass no criticisms.

George Eliot (1819–1880)

Nature teaches beasts to know their friends.
William Shakespeare (1564–1616)

Has he bit any of the children yet? If he has,
have them shot, and keep him for curiosity,
to see if it was the hydrophobia.

Charles Lamb (1775–1834)

Beautiful snow! It can do nothing wrong.
John Whittaker Watson
(1824–1890)

No cloud above, no earth below—
A universe of sky and snow.
John Greenleaf Whittier
(1807–1892)

A sad tale's best for Winter.

William Shakespeare

(1564–1616)

They talk of Christmas so long that it comes.
George Herbert (1593–1633)

Observation, not old age, brings wisdom.
Publilius Syrus
(ca. 42 B.C.)

An investment in knowledge always pays the best interest.
Benjamin Franklin (1706–1790)

Science is always wrong. It never solves a problem
without creating ten more.

George Bernard Shaw (1856–1950)

[It is a] shabby genteel sentiment . . . which makes men prefer to believe that they are degenerated angels rather than elevated apes.

William Winwood Reade (1838–1875)

I like women to let their hair
fall down their back;
'tis a most agreeable sight.
Martin Luther (1483–1546)

Every generation laughs at the old fashions,
but follows religiously the new.
Henry David Thoreau (1817–1862)

Never throw away hastily any old faith, tradition
or convention . . . they are the result of the experience
of many generations.

Sir Oliver Lodge (1851–1940)

Often would he tell the same tale in other words.
Ovid (43 B.C.?–A.D. 17)

Girls we love for what they are; young men for what
they promise to be.

Johann Wolfgang von Goethe
(1749–1832)

Adam and Eve had many advantages,
but the principal one was that
they escaped teething.

Mark Twain (1835–1910)

As our alphabet now stands, the bad spelling, or what is called so,
is generally the best, as conforming to the sound of the letters
and of the words.

Benjamin Franklin (1706–1790)

The music teacher came twice each week to bridge
the awful gap between Dorothy and Chopin.

George Ade (1866–1944)

The object of teaching a child is to enable him
to get along without his teacher.

Elbert Hubbard
(1856–1915)

They are but children too . . .
they are indeed,
children of a larger size.

Seneca
(4 B.C.?–A.D. 65)

We are always the same age inside.
Gertrude Stein
(1874–1946)

Old age, especially an honored old age, has so
great authority, that this is of more value
than all the pleasures of youth.

Marcus Cicero (106–43 B.C.)

I always think of nature as a great spectacle, somewhat resembling the opera.

Bernard de Fontenelle (1657–1757)

How wonderful opera would be
if there were no singers.

Gioacchino Rossini
(1792–1868)

To be great is to be misunderstood.
Ralph Waldo Emerson
(1803–1882)

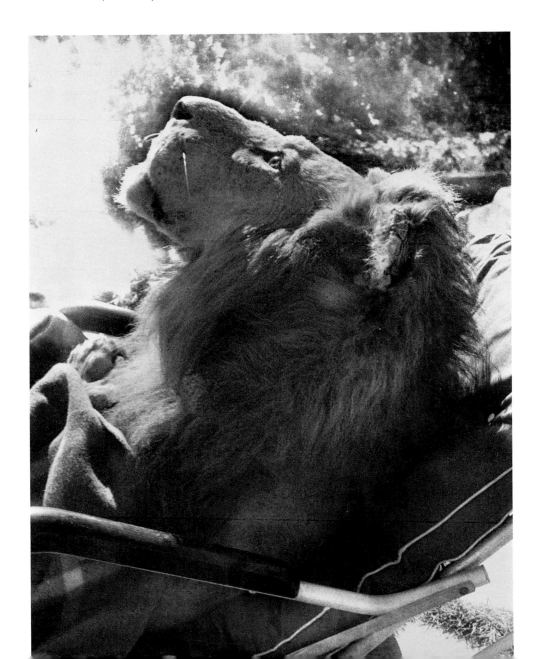

Noble blood is an accident of fortune; noble actions
are the chief mark of greatness.

Carlo Goldoni (1707–1793)

God must have loved the plain people;
he made so many of them.
Abraham Lincoln (1809–1865)

Only presidents, editors, and people with tapeworms
have the right to use the editorial "we."

Mark Twain (1835–1910)

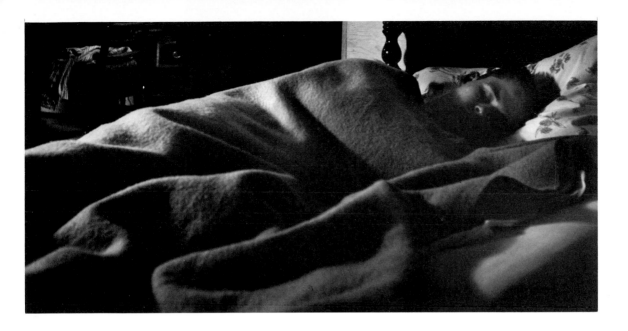

The vigorous are not better than the lazy during one-half of life for all men are alike when asleep.

Aristotle (384–322 B.C.)

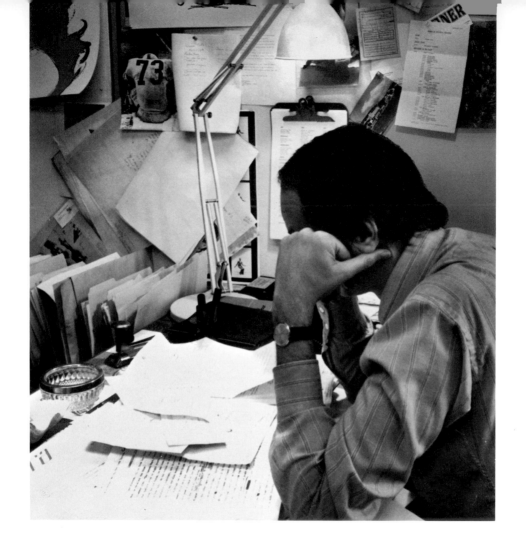

A thought comes when it wishes, not when I wish.

Friedrich Wilhelm Nietzsche
(1844–1900)

The moment one sits down to think,
one becomes all nose.

Oscar Wilde (1856–1900)

Knowledge is of two kinds. We know a subject ourselves
or we know where we can find information upon it.

Samuel Johnson (1709–1784)

Before I got married I had six theories about bringing up children; now I have six children, and no theories.

Lord Rochester (1647–1680)

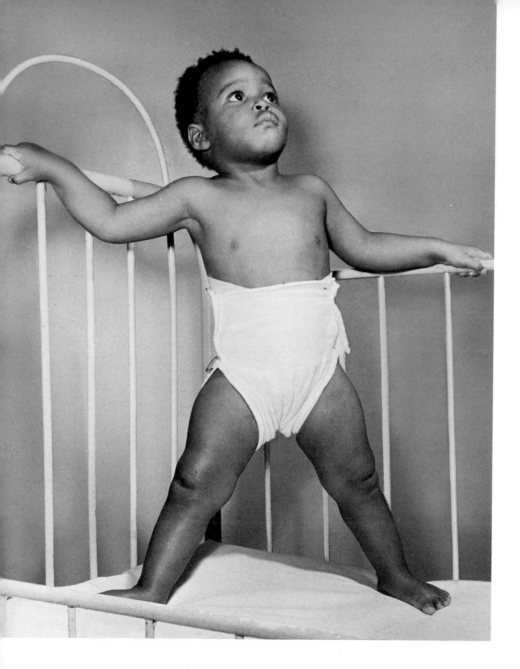

Courage may be taught as a child is taught to speak.

Euripides (480–406 B.C.)

Coolness and absence of heat and haste indicate fine qualities.

Ralph Waldo Emerson (1803–1882)

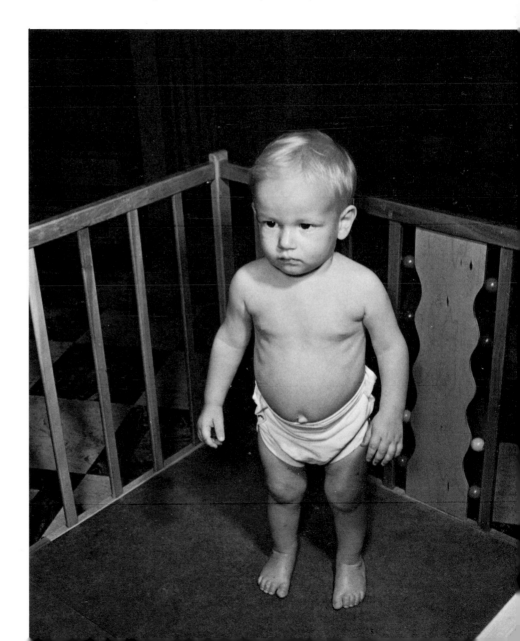

Angling may be said to be so like the mathematics that
it can never be fully learnt.

Izaak Walton (1593–1683)

Like father, like son.
William Langland
(1332?–1400)

There is nothing so good for the inside of a man as the outside of a horse.

Lord Palmerston (1784–1865)

The gray mare is the better horse.
John Heywood (1497?–1580)
(gray Flemish horses were
much valued in England in
the sixteenth century)

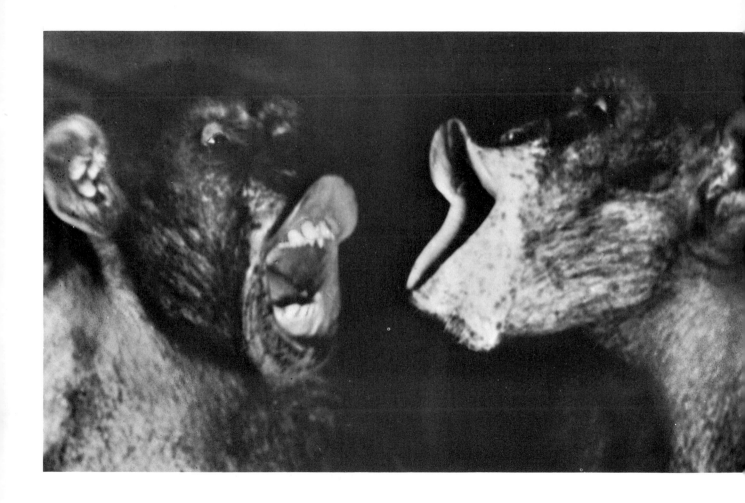

If I chance to talk a little wild, forgive me; I had
it from my father.

William Shakespeare (1564–1616)

I am not arguing with you—I am telling you.
James Abbott McNeill Whistler
(1834–1903)

The vanity of being known to be entrusted with a secret is generally one of the chief motives to disclose it.

Samuel Johnson (1709–1784)

Sooner will men hold fire in their mouths than keep a secret.
Petronius (fl. A.D. 20)

What a stranger he is who is surprised
at anything which happens in life.

Marcus Aurelius (121–180)

It is not likely that every devil does know every language . . .
'Tis possible that the education of all devils is not alike,
and that there may be some differences in their abilities.
Cotton Mather (1663–1728)

Minister had deposited the letter immediately beneath the nose
of the whole world, by way of best preventing any portion of
that world from perceiving it.

"The Purloined Letter"
Edgar Allan Poe (1809–1849)

Common sense is not so common.

Voltaire (1694–1778)

The world loves a spice of wickedness.

Henry Wadsworth Longfellow
(1807–1882)

If a man makes me keep my distance,
the comfort is he keeps his at the
same time.

Jonathan Swift
(1667–1745)

In order to compose, all you need to do is remember a tune that nobody else has thought of.

Robert Schumann (1810–1856)

You cannot put an artist's day into the life
of anyone but an artist.

Philip Gilbert Hamerton
(1834–1894)

An artist has liberty, if he is free to create
any image in any material that he chooses.
Gilbert Keith Chesterton
(1874–1936)

Fine art is that in which
the hand, the head
and the heart go together.
John Ruskin
(1819–1900)

'Tis the good reader that makes the good book.

Ralph Waldo Emerson
(1803–1882)

Some books are to be tasted,
others to be swallowed, and
some few to be chewed and digested.

Francis Bacon
(1561–1626)

You must not know too much . . . about birds
and trees and flowers . . . a certain free margin
. . . helps your enjoyment of these things.
Walt Whitman (1819–1892)

The trees are imperfect man, and seem to bemoan their imprisonment, rooted in the ground.

Ralph Waldo Emerson (1803–1882)

There is no need for man and no demand for man in nature;
it is complete without him.

William Graham Sumner (1840–1910)

Nature is perfect, wherever we look, but man always deforms it.

Friedrich von Schiller (1759–1805)

I wonder nature don't retire
From public life disgusted.
Sir William Schwenk Gilbert
(1836–1911)

The history of civilisation details the steps by which man
has succeeded in building up an artificial world within
the cosmos.

Thomas Henry Huxley (1825–1895)

Nature goes her own way, and all that to us
seems an exception is really according to order.

Johann Wolfgang von Goethe
(1749–1832)

Many demons are in woods,
in waters, in wildernesses,
and in dark pooly places.
Martin Luther (1483–1546)

The voice of one crying in the wilderness.

Isaiah (c. 740–701 b.c.)